Anything said in Latin seems profound.

Quidquid Latine dictum sit, altum videtur.

KWIHD-kwihd lah-TEE-nay DEEK-toom SIHT AHL-toom wih-DAY-toor

Are they ready for an ass whooping?

Parati sumus ad asinam verbero?

pah-RAH-tee soont AH-du Ah-zee-noma wer-bero

Are you from around here?
Are you a neighbor?

Esne vicinus?

EHS-neh wee-KEE-noos

Are you serious?

Esne serius?

EHS-neh SAY-ree-oos

Argh!

Argh!

ARGH

Art for art's sake.

Ars gratia artis.

AHRS GRAH-tee-ah AHR-this

Asswipe.

Persona non grata.

Per-SONE-a non GRART-a

As you wish.

Ut libido.

Oot lee-bee-doh

Babe!
Literally: What a cutie!

Qui pulchellus

KWEE pool-KEHL-loos

Backstabbing bastard!
Literally: and you, Brutus.

Et tu, Brute!

Eht TOO BROO-the

Behave yourself!
Act your station, Literally: Wear your success

Gere te bene!

GEH-reh TAY BEH-nay

Be still.

Vaca.

WAH-kah

Better late than never.

Melius serius quam numquam.

MEH-lee-oos SAY-ree-oos Kwahm NOOM-
kwahm

Beware of the dog

Cave canem

Cav-ay CAN-em

Brandy, Whisky
literally "water of life"

Aqua vite

Ak-wa VIT-eye

Breathe deeply.

Inspira alte.

Een-SPEE-rah AHL-tay

Bullshit
Personal attack rather than reasoned response

Ad hominem

ad HOM-in-em

Busted!
Caught red handed, flaming crime

In flagrante delicto

In flag-RANT-ay de-LICT-o

By their neglect.
A judgment given without reference to precedent.

Per incuriam

PEAR in-koor-E-yum

By the way...

Obiter...

AW-bih-tehr

Can you lend me a hand?
Can you be near me.

Potesne mihi adesse?

Paw-TEHS-neh MIH-hee ah-DEHS-she

Can't bullshit me.
Literally: I know everything.

Omnia scio.

AWM-nee-ah SKEE-oh

Carried on endlessly, To infinity

Ad infinitum

ad in-fin-EYE-tum

Cheer up!
Exhilarate

Exhila!

Ehk-SIH-lah

Chill!
Literally: Do not be tempted to.

Noli sollicitari!

NOH-lee sawl-lih-kih-TAH-ree

Chill out.
Literally: Remain Impartial

Mane aequus.

MAH-nay IGH-kwos

Come on, let's go.

Age, eamus.

AH-geh ay-AH-moos.

Could you repeat that, please?

Itera illud, si tibi placet?

IH-teh-rah IHL-lood see TIH-bee PLAH-keht

Could you spell that?

Potesne id litteris enuntiare?

Paw-TEHS-neh ihd LIHT-the-rees
ay-noon-tee-AH-reh

Count on me!
Literally: Trust me.

Confide mihi.

Kohn-FEE-deh MIH-hee

Cross your fingers.

Impone digitos alternis digitis.

Ihm-POH-neh DIH-gih-tohs ahl-TEHR-nees
DIH-gih-tees

Damn, you're ugly!

Damnare, deformis es

DAM-air-ee DE-form-ess ess

Danger in delay.

periculum in mora

pee-ree-koluma in mora

Decision was made
Die is cast

Iacta alea est

YACT-a AK-i-ya-est

Did you come by yourself?

Venistine ipse solus?

Way-nih-STEE-neh IHP-she SOH-loos

Did you know?

Cognoverasne

Kwang-noh-weh-RAHS-
neh

Done deal!

Factum negotium!

FAHK-toom neh-GOH-tee-oom

Don't give up.

Noli dedere.

NOH-lee DAY-deh-reh

Don't worry. Be happy.

Non fatigo. Sit felix.

Noan fa-tee-go SEET fa-leeks

Do what you can.

Fac is quod potes

FAHK ihd kwawd PAW-tehs

Do you mind?
Literally: Do you bear it ill will?

Fersne aegre?

FEHRS-neh IGH-gray

Dude with the boom stick!
Literally: a god out of machine

Deus ex machina!

DAY-us ex MAK-in-a

Dumb asses.
Literally: Infinite is the number of fools.

Infinitus est numerous stultorum.

Een-fee-NEE-toos ehst NOO-meh-roos
Stool-TOH-room

Eat him first!

Comedent inlum prius!

KO-may-dent een-lum pre-oh-za

Enemy of humanity in general.

Hostis humani generis

Awe-stisa OO-mani ge-na-ree-sa

Enjoy your meal!

Gaude cena tua!

GOW-day Kay-nah Too-ah

Everything comes to an end.

Omnia desinunt.

AWM-nee-ah DAY-sih-noont

Everything will be all right.
(most told lie during Zombie Apocalypse)

Omnia bona erunt

AWM-nee-ah BAW-nah EH-roont

Follow me!

Sequeris me.

SEHK-weh-rihs MAY

Forgive me.

Ignosce mihi.

Ing-NOHS-keh MIH-hee

Free as a bird.

Libera ut avis.

Lee-bah-rah oot AH-wihs

Fuck that!
Literally: Never hereafter.

Numquam posthac.

NOOM-kwahm PAWST-hahk

Full of shit.

Qui decipitur.

KWI dee-chi-pee-turrrr

Get behind me!

Vade retro!

VAR-day RET-ro

Get ready.

Para te.

PAH-rah TAY

Give me a chance.

Fac mihi potestatem.

FAHK MIH-hee paw-tehs-THAT-ehm

Give me your money. I have a catapult and will fling an enormous rock at your head.

Nisi pecuniam omnem mihi dabis, ad caput tuum saxum immane mittam

Nee-ze pea-cu-nem ahm-nem me da-bee-sa ad kaputa tomb sack-soom e-mon-eh mee-tam

Go get them, Ray!

I cape eos, Ray!

EE KAH-pah AY-ohs

Goodbye

Vale

vah-lay

Guess so.

Ut puto.

oot POO-toh

Conice?

KOHN-YIH-keh

Ave

ah-vay

Literally: Not of sound mind

Non compos mentis!

Non COM-pos MEN-tis

Help!

Succurro!

SUE-ku-rrro

Hero? Fuck that!

Heros? Ut futuis!

air-ose? Uut foo-two-e-sa

Clean version: If one must die to be recognized, I can wait.

Si post fata venit Gloria non proper

See posta fa-ta wee-nah-ta gloria noan pro-per

Holy Shit!
Literally: That's unexpected.

Id est inopinatum!

Id EHST ee-nope-ee-ah-tooma

Hold my beer.
Literally: I'd like to try it.

Id degustare velim.

Ihd day-goo-STAH-reh WEH-lihm

Honesty

Bona fides

BONE-uh FIDE-eez

How does it work?

Quo modo operator?

KWOH MAW-doh aw-peh-RAH-toor

How do you know?

Quo modo scis?

KWOH MAW-doh SKEES

How great!

Quam magnum!

Kwahm MAHNG-noom

How much is it?

Quanti est?

KWAHN-tee EHST

Hurry up!

Festina!

Fays-TEE-nah

I appreciate it.

Magni aestimo

MAHNG-nee IGH-stih-moh

I'd love to.

Velim.

WEH-lihm

I don't care.

Non mihi est curae.

NOHN MIH-hee ehst KOO-righ

I don't care about your stupid religious cult.

Nihil curo de ista tua stulta superstitione.

Knee-lu kuro di eesta two-ah stew-la-ta
super-ste-tea-own-a

I don't have time for this.

Nihil temporas mihi est.

NIH-hihl TEHM-paw-rihs MIH-hee EHST

I don't want anymore.

Nihil pluris cupio.

NIH-hihl PLOO-rihs KOO-pee-oh

I don't want it.

Id nolo.

Ihd NOH-loh

I hear

Audio

ORD-io (or) OW-di

I'll be there.

Ibi ero.

IH-bee HER-roh

I'll call you this weekend.

Hac fine septimanae te vocabo.

HAHK FEE-neh sehp-tih-MAH-nigh TAY
waw-KAW-boh

I'll do what I can.

Id quod possum faciam.

Ihd kwawd PAWS-soom FAHK-ee-ahm

I'll take it.
Literally: I'll buy it.

Id emam.

Ihd EH-mahm.

I'm a vegetarian.

Holera modo edo.

HAW-leh-rah MAW-doh EH-doh

I'm at your service.

Tibi servio.

TIH-bee SEHR-wee-oh

I'm broke.
Literally: I'm in want.

Egens sum.

AY-gayns SOOM

I'm exhausted.
Strength worn down

A viribus defectus sum.

AH WEE-rih-boos day-FEHK-toos SOOM

I'm happy for you.

Tibi laetor.

TIH-bee LIGH-tawr

I'm in a relationship.

Sponsus sum.

SPOHN-soos SOOM

I'm just looking.

Inspicio modo.

Een-SIPH-kee-oh MAW-doh

I'm looking for work in this area.

Hoc in loco operam peto.

HOHK ihn LAW-koh AW-peh-rahm PEH-toh

I'm lost.

Aberro

Ah-BEHR-roh

I'm sick.

Aegroto.

Igh-GROH-toh

I'm very sorry.
It very much sorrows me.

Me valde miseret.

MAY WAHL-day MIH-she-reht

I came, I saw, I conquered
Marlboro Cigarette?

Veni, vidi, vici

WAY-nee WEE-dee WEE-kee

I can't right now.

Nunc non possum.

NOONK nohn PAWS-soom

I don't feel like it.
It doesn't please me to do it

Id facere mihi non placet.

Ihd FAH-keh-reh MIH-hee nohn Plah-keht

I don't understand anything.
I understand nothing

Nihil intellego.

NIH-hihl ihn-TEHL-leh-goh

I like you a lot.

Multo te amo.

MOOL-toh TAY AH-moh

I love it.

Mihi placet.

MIH-hee PLAH-keht

I miss you.

Te desidero.

TAY day-SEE-deh-roh

I pity the fool!

Miseret stulte!

Me-zer-et STOOL-te

In secret
By stealth, underhanded

In clam

In klam

It's an emergency.

Discrimen est.

Dihs-KREE-mehn ehst

It's been a pleasure.

Id est in voluptate.

Id EHST een wool-PA-ta-tay

It is lunch time.

Tempus prandii est.

TEHM-poos-ah PRAHN-dee EHST

It's a beautiful day!

Amoenus dies est!

Ah-MOY-noos DEE-ays EHST

It's better this way.

Sic melius est.

SEEK MEH-lee-oos ehst.

It's on me.
Literally: My gift.

Meum donum.

MAY-oom DOH-noom

It's too hot!

Nimis calidum est!

NIH-mihs KAH-lih-doom ehst

It's your turn.

Tuus iactus est.

Too-oos YAHK-toos EHST

I love you

Te amo.

TAY AH-moh

Innocent

Tabula rasa

TAB-yool-a RAR-sa

I think, therefore I am

Cogito ergo sum

COG-it-o ER-go sum

I told you so.

Ita tibi dixi.

IH-tah TIH-bee DEEK-see

I will kill you with this shovel!

Et percutiam te cum hoc ligonem

a-et per-coo-ti-um te kuma ah-K LEE-go-nim

It's too big for me.
Author Note: I hear this all the time.

Nimis magna est quoniam mihi.

Nee-mis MAGH-na EHST kwan-yuam mee

Ad ipsum temporis.

Ahd IHP-soom TEHM-paw-rihs

Semel tantum.

SHE-mehl THAN-toom

Literally: Brutal lightning

Brutum fulmen!

Bru-tooma fool-mena

Know thyself.

Nosce te ipsum.

NOH-skeh TAY IHP-soom

Leave it alone!

Stet

Stet

Leave me alone.

Desere me.

Day-SHE-reh MAY

Let there be light

Fiat lux

FEE-at lux

Let justice be done though the heavens fall.

Fiat justitia ruat caelum

Fee-at Jus-tech-ee-ah roo-AHT KY-luma

Let's go dancing.

Eamus chorum.

Ay-AH-moos Sha-room

Let's go drinking.

Eamus ad bibendum.

Ay-AH-moos ahd Bih-BEHN-doom

Let's go for a walk.

Eamus ambulatum.

Ay-AH-moos ahm-boo-LAH-toom

Let's see if we are lucky.

Decernamus an fortunate simus.

Day-kehr-NAH-moos ahn fawr-too-NAH-tee
SEE-moos

Let the buyer beware.

Caveat emptor.

KAH-way-aht AYMP-tawr

Life is beautiful.

Vita pulchra est.

WEE-tah POOL-krah ehst

Live and learn.
Literally: Experiences teaches.

Experientia docet.

Ehk-speh-ree-EHN-tee-ah DAW-keht

Live and let live.

Vive et sine vivere.

Wee-weh eht SIH-neh WEE-weh-reh

Live for today!
Choose the day! Seize the Day!

Carpe diem!

KAHR-peh DEE-ehm

Look!

Specta!

SPEHK-tah

Look it's Elvis

Ecce illud Elvis

Eh-chi elu-dah Elvis

Love conquers all

Amore vincit Omnia

AH-mawr WIHN-kiht AWM-nee-ah

Love is the essence of life.

Amor est vitae essential.

AH-mawr EHST WEE-tigh ehs-SEHN-tee-ah

Made Up, Improvised
literally "to this"

Ad hoc

ad-hok

Making love out of nothing at all.

Clinopale de nihil omnino

KLEE-no-pail dee nih-hee ahm-ne-no

May I help you?

Quo modo tibi opem ferre possum?

KWOH MAW-doh TIH-bee AW-pehm FEHR-reh
PAWS-soom

My fault

Mea culpa

MAY-ah KOOL-pah

My precious.

Meus pretiosum.

Mez pray-ti-oh-suma

My Turn!

Iactus meus est!

YAHK-toos MAY-oos ehst

Nobody's home.

Nemo intus est.

NAY-moh IHN-toos ehst.

No punishment without a law.

Nulla poena sine lege.

New-la PO-ain-ah see-ne lay-J

No way!
Literally: I forbid.

Veto

VEE-tow

Oh, hell no!

O, non inferno!

OH non en-FER-no

OK

Rectus es

RAYK-toos ehs

Pay attention!
Literally: Do what you are doing.

Age quod agis!

Ah-je KWOD a-geez

Please

si placet

see PLAH-chet

Quiet!

Consedo!

Kown-say-dogh

Red or White Wine?

Russum aut album vinum?

ROOS-soom owt AHL-boom WEE-noom

Rest.
Literally: Go lie down.

I cubitum

EE KOO-bih-toom

Rest in Peace

Requiescat in pace

Rek-wi-ES-cat in par-kay

Run!

Curro!

Koo-rrrow

Same shit different day.
Literally: The state in which things are

Staus quo

State-us kwo

See! Dumb ass.
Idiot. By the fact itself

Stultus es. Ipso facto.

stool-tas ess. IP-so FACT-o.

Seeing is believing.

Id tibi videndum est ut credas.

Ihd TIH-bee wih-DEHN-doom ehst oot KRAY-dahs

Shit don't add up.
Literally: Does not follow, broken argument

Non sequiter

Non SEK-wit-er

Snake in the grass.

Anguis in herba.

AHN-gwihs ihn HEHR-bah

So far so good.

Adhuc bonum.

AHD-hook BAW-noom

Sometimes

Interdum

Ihn-TEHR-doom

Sorry

ignosce mihi

een-YOH-shay MEE-hee

Starving.

Esurio.

Ay-SOOR-ee-oh

Stay Calm.

Mora tranquillo

Mor-ah TRAN-kwi-lo

Step by step.
Literally: He suffered his stride

Passus passu.

PAHS-soos PAHS-soo

Step by step.
Literally: step by step

Quasi per gradus.

KWA-zi per GRA-deus-ah

Strange but true.

Mirum sed verum.

MEE-room sehd WAY-room

Sucks to be you.
Literally: very unlucky

Valde infelix.

WAHL-day een-FAY-leeks

Take a breather.

Remitte te.

Reh-MIHT-the TAY

Take care of yourself!

Cura te!

KOO-rah TAY

Take that, bitches!

Inlido ubi sunt canes.

Een-lee-do oo-bee soon kan-ess-uh

Thank You

gratias tibi ago

GRAH-tee-as Ti-bee Ah-goh

That's all.

Id totum est.

Ihd TOH-toom ehst.

That's crazy!

Absurdum est!

Ahps-SOOR-doom ehst

Therefore

Ergo

UR-go

That's life.
Such is life

Tale est vita.

TAH-leh ehst WEE-tah

Think before you act.
Literally: Think before you leap.

Cogita ante salis.

KOH-gih-tah AHN-the SAH-lees

This is crap-ola!
Literally: It is very cheap

Vilissimum est.

Wee-LIHS-sih-moom EHST

This is my wife.
Literally: Behold my wife

Ecce maritum maritam meam.

EHK-keh mah-REE-toom mah-REE-tahm
May-ahm.

This way, please.

Huc, si placet.

HOOK see PLAH-keht

Time flies!

Tempus fugit!

TEHM-poos FOO-giht

Time to move on.

Tempus progredi.

Tim-poos PRO-gray-dee

Tit for tat.
Something for something

Quid pro quo.

KWIHD proh KWOH

Truth never dies.

Veritas nunquam perit.

WAY-rih-tahs NOOM-kwahm pehr-eet

Use the force!

Uti tu vis!

OO-ti too wee

Voice of the people
We said so

Vox populi

Vox POP-yool-ee

Watch out!

Exspecta!

Ehk-SPEHK-tah

We are leaving.

Nos relinquere

NOS ray-lean-kware-lay

We get along great.

Bene nos habemus.

BEH-neh NOHS hah-BAY-moos

We have a problem.

Aerumnam habemus.

Igh-ROOM-nahm hah-BAY-moos

Welcome

Salve

Sal-vay

Well done!

Bene factum!

BEH-neh FAHK-toom

What a shame (pity).

Quantum miserandum est.

KWAHN-toom mih-she-RAHN-doom EHST

What a surprise!

Quod miratus.

KWAWD MEE-rah-toos

What are your plans?

Qualia sunt consilia tua.

KWAH-lee-ah soont kohn-SIH-lee-ah
Too-ah

What do I do?
Literally: What is to be done by me.

Quid est mihi faciendum

KWIHD EHST MIH-hee fahk-kee-EHN-doom

What do you do?

Quid agis?

KWIHD AH-gihs

What else?

Quid aliud?

KWIHD ah-loo-da

What happened?

Quid factum est?

KWIHD FAHK-toom ehst

What's done is done.

Quod factum est, id factum est.

Kwawd FAHK-toom ehst, IHD FAHK-toom ehst.

What is this?

Quid est hoc?

KWIHD EHST HOHK.

What time do they open?
Literally: When are they ready to do business?

Ubi ad negotiandum parati sunt?

OO-bee ahd neh-goh-tee-AHN-doom pah-
RAH-tee soont

What time is the game?

Quota hora est ludus?

KWOH-tah HOH-rah EHST LOO-doos

When is your birthday?

Ubi est dies natalis tuus?

OO-bee ehst DEE-ays nah-TAH-lihs TOO-oos

When will it end?

Quando finibit?

KWAHN-doh fee-NEE-biht

Where are you going?

Quo vadis?

Kwo VAD-is

Where shall we meet?

Ubi convenemus?

OO-bee kawn-weh-NAY-moos

Who guards the guards?

Quis custodiet ipsos custodies?

Kwis cus-TOAD-ee-yet IP-soss cus-Toad-ez

Who is that?

Quis est, qui?

KWIS est KWI

Without a doubt.

Sine dubio.

SIH-neh DOO-bee-oh

You ain't gonna believe this shit!
Literally: I believe it because it is absurd

Credo quia absurdum est.

Kree-do kwi-ah ab-zur-du est

You earned it!

Id meruisti.

Ihd meh-roo-IH-stee

You're late.

Serus es.

SAY-roos EHS

You know what's cool? Zombies.

Scitis quod est impudens? Mortuorum
Ambbulantum.

She-tis kwad ist IM-poo-dance-ah
More-twar-oom ahm-boo-lan-tooma

You must have the body.

Habeas corpus

HABE-e-as CORP-us

Your mother is rotten!
Mama is worm dirt.

Mater est ubi vermis terra cibum!

Your shoe's untied

Calceamenta solvate est

Zombie!

Mortus vivens!

MORE-toos Wee-wen-sa

Yes	certe	(CHAIR-tay)
No	non	(noan)
No	nullo	NUL-loh Mo-doh
Who	quis?	KWISS
What	quid?	kwid
Where	ubi? Quo?	OO-bee (or) kwo
Why	cur?	KOOR
When	quom?	kwom
Which	quod?	kwod
How many	quot?	Kw-oat
What Kind?	qualis?	KWA-liss
Sunday	dies Solis	SAW-liss
Monday	dies Lunae	loo-NIGH
Tuesday	dies Martis	MAR-tee-zus
Wednesday	dies Mercurii	mer-KUR-ee
Thursday	dies Iovis	loo-vees
Friday	dies Veneris	WEH-neh-rihs
Saturday	dies Saturni	SA-tur-knee

Yesterday	heri	aire
Today	hodie	aw-dee-eh
Tomorrow	cras	krass
Never	nunquam	noon-kwam
Always	semper	sim-per
Perhaps	forte, fortasse	four-tay
Maybe	fortasse, forte	for-tass-eh

I hope you enjoyed the book and thanks.

Tusitala – Songs of a Sailor, Nov 2013 is a book of poetry, lyrics and art derived from thirty years of my life's experiences.

Trenchant – A Pirate's Journal, Jan 2014 is a book about leaning life's experiences through the readers interactive writings as a young new pirate crew member.

Casey - Don't Ever Call Me Worthless, Jan 2013 Is the prequel to **A Life Worthwhile**, both books are about Romance and the love and acceptance a man offers his soul mate, a person who suffers with a mental illness. The third and final installment of this Trilogy is **Justice For None** planned for a June 2014 release it will be offered as soon as it is fact checked and ready.

Works in progress. Look for them soon.

Saving America, projected Jan 2015. Real solutions to problems facing America and absolutely no plan for a zombie apocalypse in it.

Fiendishly Fancy Fare, projected Sept 2014, is a Halloween Cook Book concocted from the Orr Family Tradition of Feasting on Halloween.

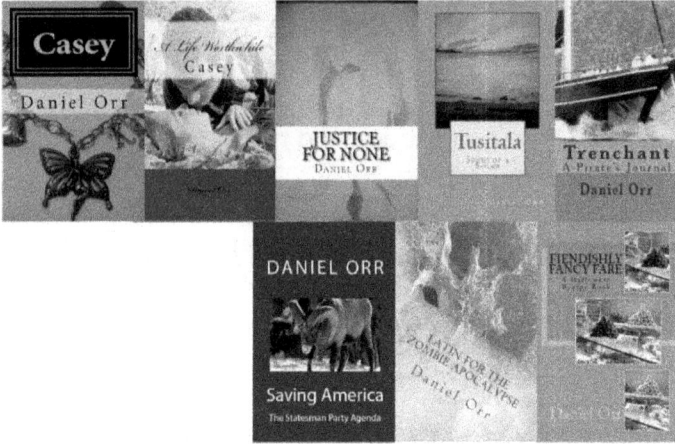

*** Don't forget to leave a book review on Amazon.com or BarnesandNoble.com

Feel free to tell me your thoughts or share your experiences with me. DanielOrr@nc.rr.com